"REVENOOERS", see page 36.

CARVING FIGURE CARICATURES
in the Ozark Style

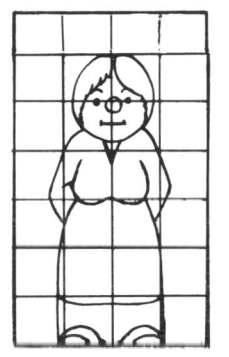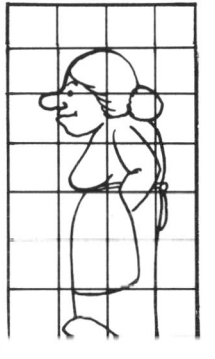

HAROLD L. ENLOW

WITH 22 DRAWINGS
AND 47 PHOTOGRAPHS
BY WADE RADFORD
AND THE AUTHOR

DOVER PUBLICATIONS, INC., NEW YORK

Published in Canada by General Publishing
Company, Ltd., 30 Lesmill Road, Don Mills,
Toronto, Ontario.
Published in the United Kingdom by Constable
and Company, Ltd., 10 Orange Street, London
WC 2.

Carving Figure Caricatures in the Ozark Style
is a new work, first published by Dover Publications, Inc., in 1975.

International Standard Book Number: 0-486-23151-8
Library of Congress Catalog Card Number: 74-17879

Manufactured in the United States of America
Dover Publications, Inc.
180 Varick Street
New York, N. Y. 10014

Foreword

Over the past few years, wood carving has become very much a part of the Ozarks. Each wood carver has his or her own specialty and way of doing things. Some carve beautiful plaques or birds, some prefer carving horses or other animals and still others just like to sit under a shade tree and whittle away on a stick. I carve caricatures, some Ozarkian and some from who-knows-where, striving to capture something in each one which will bring a smile or chuckle to all who see them.

Perhaps this book will be a help to all carvers (or carvers-to-be) who like to see people smile too.

H. L. E.

Dogpatch Wood Carving
Dogpatch, Arkansas
May, 1974

RUFUS and SADIE, see page 27.

Acknowledgments

I would like to extend my appreciation to the following people for their help in the preparation of this book:

My friend, Wade Radford, for taking many of the photographs and giving general advice;

My wife, Elaine, for correcting and typing the manuscript;

All my wood-carving friends, from whom I have learned many things, some of which are included herein.

Special thanks to Ida Engler and Peter Engler for helping to make wood carving a part of the Ozarks, by the encouragement they have given so many carvers.

MISSOURI MULE, see page 10.

Contents

[Additional carvings by the author are found on pp. 38-39.]

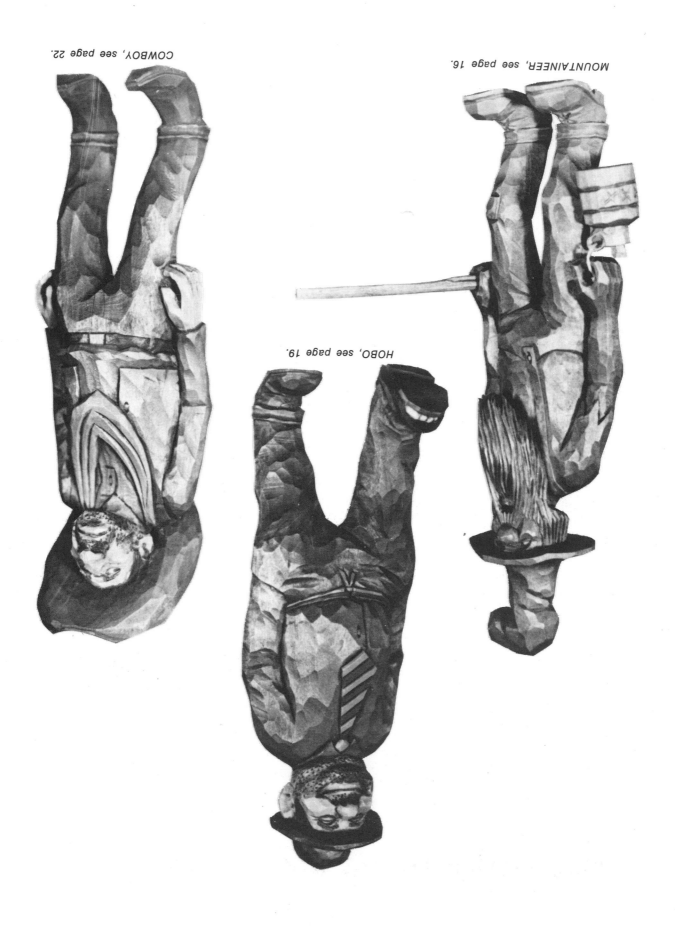

COWBOY, see page 22.

HOBO, see page 19.

MOUNTAINEER, see page 16.

Selecting and Preparing the Wood

WHICH WOOD TO USE

Most carvers use woods which are nearby and readily available; a carver is lucky if he has good carving wood in his back yard. Not all carvers are this lucky, however, and many must learn what kind of wood to be on the lookout for.

In the Ozark country, where I live, basswood or lindenwood ("linn" to old-timers) is the standby for carving. It is ideal for small carvings of people and animals, especially caricatures. Other woods used, especially for larger projects, are sassafras, black walnut, butternut and red cedar. But I would advise the beginning carver to get linden if he or she possibly can.

In my area linden is usually purchased from small mountain sawmills, the tree usually having been cut only a few days before being sawed into planks.

PREPARING WOOD FOR CARVING

The primary step in preparing wood for carving—whether linden or any other wood—is getting it sufficiently dry. Since most carvers have no kiln in which to dry it, it must be stacked and stripped. Stripping means putting small, inch-thick pieces of wood between the planks so that air will circulate between them.

If the planks are allowed to dry through the ends instead of the sides and edges, long cracks will appear and ruin a good part of each piece. Ends should therefore be coated with melted paraffin to keep moisture from escaping. Use extreme caution when melting the paraffin; put the wax in a clean coffee can, then allow it to melt in a pan of hot water. **Do not** melt over a direct flame. Use an old paint brush to apply the melted paraffin to the ends of each plank.

After coating the ends, store stacked wood in a dry place for several weeks before carving. Drying time depends largely upon the thickness of the wood, but for the small projects in this book, which use 2- to 3-inch planks, drying time is about six weeks. Logs cut in winter months dry faster and work better; sap is down and there is less moisture in them at that time of year.

Selecting the Proper Tools

THE BASIS FOR SELECTION

Many carving tools of good quality are available on today's market, and the purchaser could well be confused by the sheer variety of them. My own tool box contains several different brands, since I have experimented over the years with various tools, looking for different characteristics. Actually, there are two basic criteria for choosing tools: good design and ability to hold an edge.

Many beginners fail to realize that most carving tools are sold unsharpened—one hates to think how many carvers have given up after trying unsharpened tools. Sharpening will be discussed in the next chapter—it is probably the most important fact for the beginning carver. Most of the time when a tool doesn't cut properly, it isn't because of the tool itself but because of improper sharpening.

TOOL HANDLES

A good tool always has a shoulder where it enters the handle to keep it from splitting the handle wood. Tool handles should be of very hard wood, and the larger tools should have a ferrule or metal banding where the handle attaches to the tool. Handles for extra-heavy work should be banded at both ends.

Most small and medium tools are sold with handles attached; large tools and their handles, however, usually are sold separately. You will have to know how to attach the handle if you purchase them separately. Many tools have been broken because the handle was forced on. Tool handles have a pre-drilled hole, ready to accept the tool. Twist the tang of the tool into the handle, using a back-and-forth motion, so that the tool drills its way in. Continue until the tool is about 1/4 inch from being seated. Then place it on a block of wood and drive the final quarter-inch with a wooden mallet.

Since a bent tool is easily broken, do not drive the handle in on a block of wood. When it is twisted in, place the shank of the tool in a vise between two blocks of wood, then pound on the handle.

SUBSTITUTION AND NUMBER OF TOOLS

While, as we said, many tools are available today, it is doubtful that you, as a beginner, will need more than a few of them. As you progress you will find a need for other tools, depending upon the type of carving you are doing. If you are a professional carver, of course, you will discover many tools that will save you time and energy if applied to problem areas.

To recognize different tools easily, some carvers like to paint the handles different colors. This will eliminate searching for particular tools, as you will learn to know each by its color.

Each of the ten projects in this book will list the tools being used, to give the reader some idea of which tools made the different cuts. Don't be afraid to substitute if you think the same results may be obtained by using a different tool.

MAKING YOUR OWN TOOLS

If you think you would like making your own tools, this is possible also, and adds to the fun of carving. Old files and broken cross-cut saw blades are excellent metals for making your own tools. Try to pick pieces of metal you know were originally from hard-edge tools. Use a power grinder to shape metal into the tool shape desired, being careful not to get the metal hot. Keep a can of water near you and dunk the tool occasionally, since an overheated tool will not hold an edge. If overheating does occur, or if you need to heat the tool for bending, it may be tempered again by heating the tool cherry-red and quenching in cold water.

Care of Tools: Sharpening

MATERIALS FOR SHARPENING

Practically every book written on wood carving has a chapter on sharpening, and rightly so, for this is the most important thing the beginner needs to know. Sharpening is a science in itself, not difficult to learn, although it does take time and patience. We will go over the process briefly, so as not to confuse the reader with too much detail. If you know an experienced tool sharpener, watching him at work is a good way to learn the method.

To begin, you will need a Carborundum stone with coarse and fine sides, a hard Arkansas stone (a hard Arkansas slipstone will be needed for the inside of the v-tool) and a piece of smooth cowhide for stropping your tools (see Fig. 1). Any size cowhide will do, but I use a piece two inches wide by twelve inches long. For ease in using, the cowhide may be glued onto a piece of wood, or you may want to use a razor strop if one is available. It is up to the individual whether he or she wants to use honing compound on the leather. Personally, I prefer the use of a fine abrasive; jeweler's rouge will work as well if a compound isn't available.

SHARPENING KNIVES

We will start with a common knife blade and the coarse side of the Carborundum stone. Apply some light oil (kerosene works well) to make the stone cut better and also keep the stone from becoming clogged. Do not use linseed oil, as it will dry on your stone and cause clogging.

Lay the blade flat on the stone, then raise the back of the blade slightly, about 1/16 inch (see Fig.

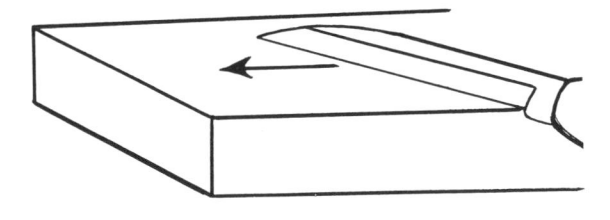

Fig. 1a.   Knife blade being pushed on the stone.

1a). Push the blade back and forth the length of the stone, applying pressure all the while. If the knife is a folding type (such as a pocket knife), apply pressure only when pushing (that is, edge first), otherwise it will fold on your hand. You will feel the stone cutting the metal as you go through this procedure. This pushing, pulling and applying pressure will have to be continued on both sides of

the blade until the edge becomes sharp. When you think the edge is sharp, test with your thumbnail. If it is sharp, it will catch on your nail, digging in. If it is not yet sharp, it will slide off your nail and the sharpening on the coarse side of the stone must continue. Test all along the blade for sharpness, especially out near the point.

When the blade is sharp, turn the Carborundum over, and repeat the process on the fine side of the stone. You will not need to apply much pressure here as you are only striving to make the sharpened edge a little finer. It should only take a few strokes. Next, use the hard Arkansas stone; this will put an even finer edge on the blade. Put a few drops of oil on the Arkansas also, and repeat the same process as you did on the Carborundum. You will see the sides of the blade getting shiny as you hone.

When you feel you have honed your blade very well, you may use the strop (Fig. 1b). Since the

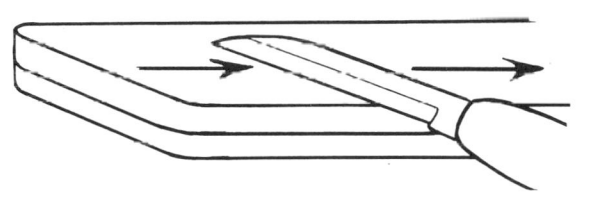

Fig. 1b.   Stropping a knife blade on leather.

strop is leather, don't push the blade, or it will cut the leather. Strop it as the barber strops his razor, by pulling. A few pulls on the strop are all that is necessary. Too much stropping will round the edge on your knife. In using leather, be sure to use the smooth side for stropping, since the coarse side will dull your tools.

If you have sharpened the blade as described, your knife should shave hair off your arm. If it does not, something is wrong. Either you don't have it quite sharp enough or the knife is made of inferior steel and will not take this kind of edge.

The bevel, or that part of the blade from which the metal has been ground away, is important to good carving. Wider bevels on the sides of the blade will make it cut more smoothly. Ideally, this bevel will show on the entire side of the blade. This wide bevel is accomplished by laying the blade flat on the stone when sharpening.

When carving on very hard woods, the tools aren't beveled quite so much, as they will break easily. I rarely carve hard woods (by this I do not mean the hardwood family), and so prefer long bevels on my knives.

SHARPENING CHISELS

Chisels are sharpened like knife blades, using the same pushing and pulling method on the Carborundum and hard Arkansas stone (Fig. 1c), and pulling or stropping on the leather. Chisels may be beveled on one side or both sides; this is a matter of individual preference. If you are going to carve softer woods and prefer a long bevel, by all means make it long.

If you sharpen only one side and a little burr forms along the edge, turn the chisel over, lay the flat side on the stone and push a couple of times. This should remove the burr.

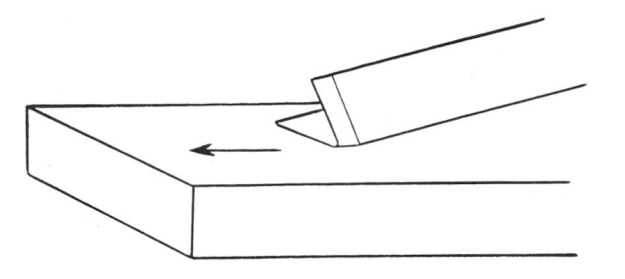

Fig. 2a. Sharpening a v-tool on the stone.

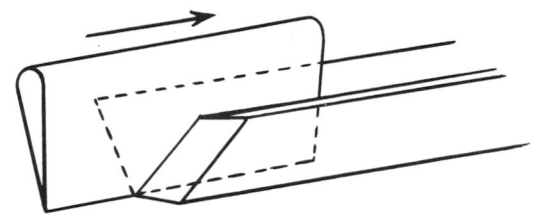

Fig. 2b. Deburring inside of the v-tool on Arkansas slipstone.

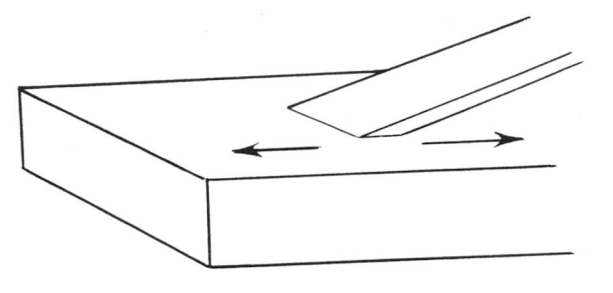

Fig. 1c. Position for sharpening a chisel on the stone.

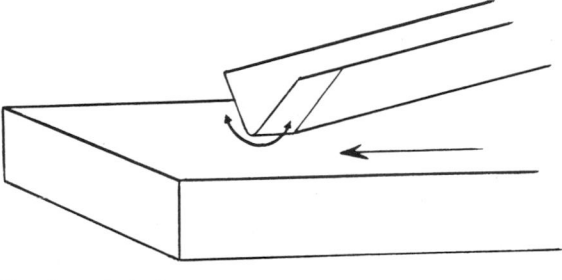

Fig. 2c. Rubbing off point of the v-tool.

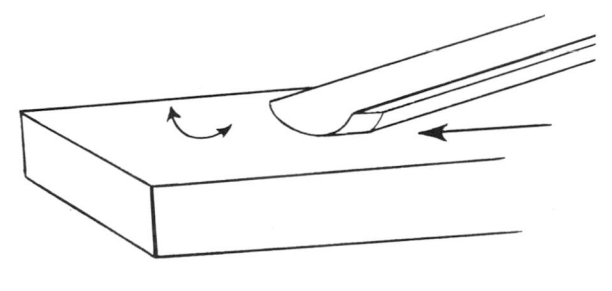

Fig. 1d. Sharpening a gouge on a flat stone.

SHARPENING GOUGES

Gouges are a little more difficult to sharpen, especially if you have only a flat stone. It is for this that an Arkansas slipstone is needed. While pushing and pulling the gouge on the stones, you must move it from side to side so it will be beveled and sharp all around (see Fig. 1d). Most gouges are sharpened only on the outside, but you may bevel the inside somewhat if desired. If you have a slipstone, it will take the burrs from the inside of your gouges. Remember to rotate the gouge as you strop, so it will be keen all around the edge.

SHARPENING V-TOOLS

These tools are easy to sharpen, if you know one little trick, and that is how to sharpen the point properly. Sharpen each side of the v-tool first, as if you were sharpening a chisel (Fig. 2a). Burrs on the

inside can be removed with a small slipstone (Fig. 2b). After both sides of the V are nice and keen, the point must be sharpened to conform to the way the tool is ground inside (Fig. 2c). The tip should not be like a point at all, but more like a tiny gouge; this procedure we will call rubbing off the point. The v-tool (including the inside) should also be stropped, if you have access to a smooth wedge of leather. Some sculpture-houses sell these wedges and a commercial honing compound, but you may want to cut your own leather wedge.

Two final reminders: sharpening should not be taken too lightly; work hard at it until you get it right. This could very well make the difference between quality work and shoddy-looking pieces. Remember, too, that the tool marks left on the work show that it is hand-carved, so be proud of them. Caricatures should not be sanded smooth.

A WORD OF CAUTION

Now that I have shown you how to sharpen properly, I must warn you, too, to use extreme care when carving. Always handle tools very carefully, as they can cut one's hands, legs, and other parts of the body, as well as wood.

Avoid carving towards the body. Do not put one hand in front of your tool while pushing with the other. The index finger always seems to be in the way, and is a likely target.

Train yourself to keep both hands behind the cutting edge of any tool. With large pieces of work, and large tools, try clamping your work or putting it in a vise. This will eliminate your holding it with one hand which might get in the way. The best procedure is to use the mallet when possible.

You will probably amaze yourself with the dexterity you develop in your hands. As you carve, you will notice using your left thumb as a fulcrum on the back of your knife blade if you are right-handed, or using your right thumb if you are left-handed. This seems to come naturally, after a little practice. Most carvers rely heavily on their thumbs; they add the strength and control needed when carving.

Even if you are very cautious, you are sure to get nicked occasionally. It's easy to get so carried away with a wood carving that you will forget to be careful, but this is all part of carving. Adhesive bandages are a good item to have in that tool box. If you do nick yourself, but not too seriously, just keep working; this will keep the nick from getting sore.

The Carver's Mallet

A mallet can prove quite useful. Used with a gouge or other large tool, it is good for roughing out large figures. Here it will save you much time and labor, so use it whenever possible. If you can clamp down your small carvings, you can use the mallet and large tools on them also, especially for the roughing out.

Always use the mallet with caution, as it will break tools and handles if used incorrectly. Do not swing the mallet like a baseball bat, but rather use a swing of a few inches. You may need a little more swing than that in certain difficult areas, but do use care. When roughing out hard woods with a mallet, use smaller tools than you would on soft woods. By switching to smaller tools, you will lessen your swing.

What you can do with the mallet may be surprising; besides roughing, or doing work on large carvings, you may also put it to its best use on detail work. If you tap the tool delicately with the mallet, you can carve with surprising precision. While you are doing this finer work, the hand holding the tool should not push but only guide. Let the mallet do all the work, and you can tap the tool to the exact spot you intend, without ever worrying about your tool slipping. Learn to use the mallet with ease; using it will take less effort than you think, particularly if you learn to relax.

Use of the Band Saw in Wood Carving

To remove excess wood and save yourself time, you may saw the outline of your figure either with a coping saw or with a band saw. If you have access to a band saw, always practice extreme safety when using it or any other power tool. Do not put fingers and thumbs directly in front of the blade, but place hands so that if a slip is made, your hands will go on either side of the blade. Try resting the heel of your hands on the top or edge of the saw table, pushing with your fingers and thumbs. This way, you will have more control than if you are pushing with your arms and shoulders.

It is seldom necessary to turn sharp corners with a band saw. You can avoid turns if you make cuts from different angles, taking out chunks of wood here and there until you have the wooden form completed. This will save wear and tear on saw blades, and they will last much longer.

If a block of wood becomes stuck in the blade, stop the saw. Put something firm against the blade to hold it in place, and pull the block loose. Sometimes you can loosen the wood by jiggling it or wedging a screwdriver in the cut to spread the wood apart.

An important warning: **do not** wear loose clothing when using power tools, as it can easily become entangled in the saw, causing serious injury or accident.

Roughing Out a Figure from a Block

If you do not have a power saw to rough out the figure you wish to carve, there are other ways of doing this. You may rough out the figure in your lap, using only your knife; however, this is the hard way. The easiest way is to use a fairly large gouge or chisel, and let a clamp or vise hold the piece while the excess wood is removed. Here is basically how this may be accomplished.

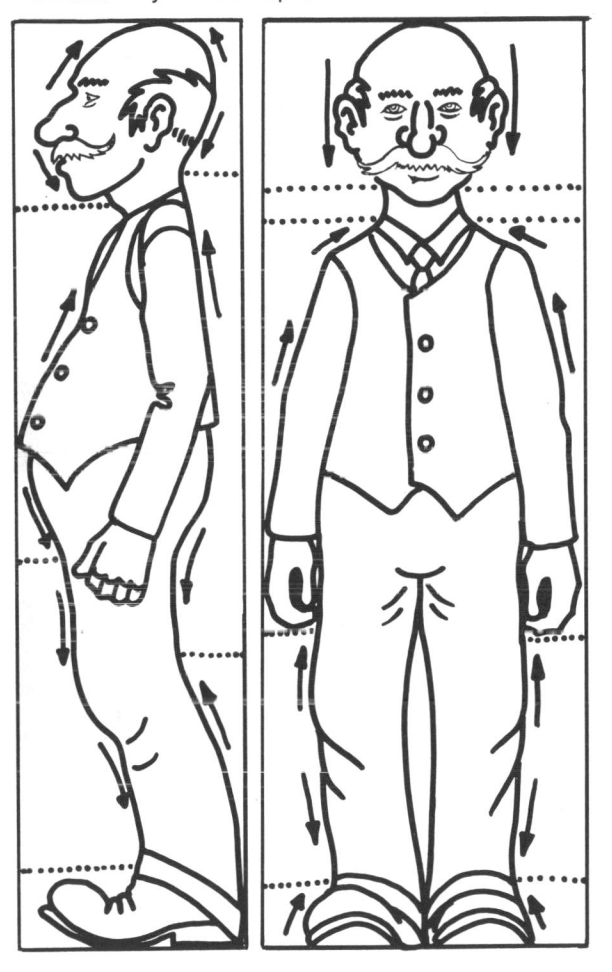

Fig. 3. Illustration of old-timer. Dotted lines show where to make the cross–grain saw cuts when starting with a block. Arrows show direction for cutting with a gouge and mallet, to be used if band saw is not available.

Draw a side view of the figure, either human or animal, which you are going to carve on the block of wood, or trace it from a pattern, using a sheet of tracing paper and then a sheet of carbon paper. The procedure for carving animals will be dealt with later, in Project No. 1; here we will show how to carve a human caricature (Fig. 3).

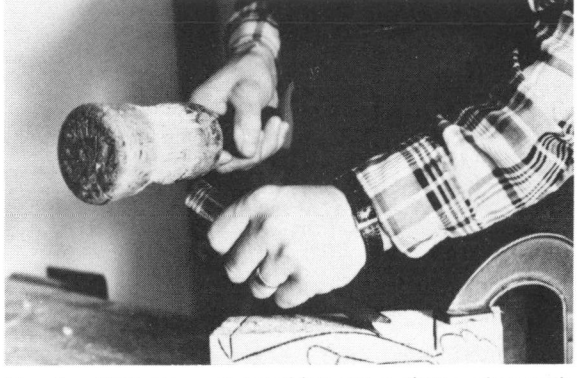

Fig. 4. First stage of roughing out a figure after making preliminary cuts with the handsaw.

Fig 5. Second stage of removing wood by hand.

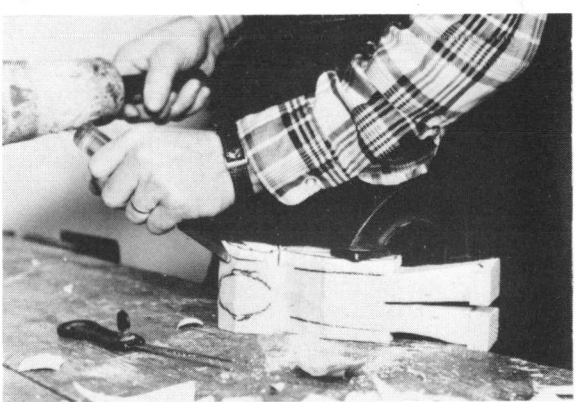

Fig. 6. Wood being removed from the sides of the head.

Using a handsaw, cut in just under the chin, just above the feet and at the back of the knee—wherever the cutting is across the grain. The dotted lines in Fig. 3 show where to saw. Next, with the work held fast, use a mallet and gouge (or chisel) to cut all the excess wood away from the front and back, so you are left with a profile. Fig. 4 shows the

7

Fig. 7. Using a wide–angled v–tool to remove excess wood in front of the arms.

Fig. 8. Removing excess wood from the sides of the head which is turned to one side. Note the shape of the head drawn on top.

block with the profile drawn on, the saw cuts already made and the first chip being chiseled away. Fig. 5 shows work progressing on the back of the figure.

Draw on the front view now, making saw cuts, then cut the wood away here as you did on the side view. As a last step, you may saw the wood from between the legs if you like, as this wood is hard to remove by any other means. Fig. 6 shows the wood

sawed from between the legs and the wood being removed from the sides.

With all this wood cut away, you are ready to proceed to the details. (Carving faces and features will be explained in a later chapter.)

Figs. 7 and 8 show preliminary roughing out of a band-sawed figure of a woman, using a large v-tool and chisel.

Finishing Your Carvings

PAINT FINISHES

Many carvers have only the vaguest idea of how to finish a carving. To help them, each project listed in the remainder of the book will give detailed instructions for finishing. Variations are encouraged, however, and any finish used on one project may just as well be used on any other.

For my own carvings I prefer a soft finish, rather than a high-gloss or harshly colored one. For some years, I used the white gas and oil paint method; that is, using tube oil colors, I mixed in enough white gas and thinned to the desired color. Similar to a stain, it dried very rapidly and gave a nice subdued color.

I no longer use this method, however, because of the danger and the smell of the fumes. Water colors, such as those found in inexpensive sets for children, will give you the same effect on colored or polychromed carvings. If you are going to do a good deal of painting, however, tube water colors will prove economical, whereas a small set will have colors you will never use, while there will be other colors you will need more often. Colors I principally use include emerald green, cadmium yellow, yellow ochre, lamp black, cobalt blue, raw umber, vermilion and a bright red. For white, I use acrylic, as it will cover the surface more easily than the water color; it, too, is thinned with water. Or you may want to use all acrylic paints; if so, you will have to work rapidly or the paint will dry too fast and cause streaking.

After letting the paint dry for about an hour, umber antiquing may be used on either the water colors or the acrylics. Wipe off the excess at once, leaving some in the cracks and low spots to give an appearance of something very old.

Another popular finish is raw umber oil paint, thinned with raw linseed oil. (Do not use raw umber **water** paint; make sure this is oil paint.) Add linseed oil until the desired stain is obtained, then test on a scrap of wood, adding more linseed oil if it is too dark and more oil paint if it is too light. You will soon know the right mixture of each. Brush the carving thoroughly with this stain, and wipe off any excess; it may take several days to dry completely. The finish is similar in appearance to the finish on some German carvings I have seen, and gives a very rich look to your work.

NATURAL FINISH

If you want to leave your carving natural, first clean the carving of any soiled places, either by sanding very lightly or scrubbing with soap and water. If you scrub it, do not allow it to soak, and be sure to let it dry overnight. Then apply a coat of clear shellac. When this is dry, you may use steel wool lightly, and apply a coat of paste floor wax. After allowing this to dry for an hour, buff with a soft cloth or a polishing brush. Do not wait too long to buff, as the wax will get a whitish look, which will be hard to eliminate. This finish is especially attractive on a grained wood, although I use it on basswood at times.

STAINS

Many commercial stains are available, in about any color you might want. A favorite of mine is knotty-pine, a soft, light, brownish color. When I stain a carving, I always finish by waxing and buffing, as I do on a natural carving.

Basswood takes any of these finishes well. Often a walnut stain will soak in and become too dark on basswood, depending upon the brand of stain. If you are going to try out any stain, always test it first on a scrap of the type of wood you are planning to stain.

I never color the beautifully grained woods, such as walnut or sassafras, but usually leave them natural.

A good piece of work is often ruined by an improper finish. Of course, getting the right finish for the right piece of work comes with practice and a good bit of trial and error.

A WORD TO THE CARVER

I have not gone into a great deal of detail about woods, tools, and the like, because there are many excellent wood-carving books from which this information is available.

My main purpose is to answer many of the questions people frequently ask, principally by showing you how I do it; as I stated before, however, try your own methods. If you like your way better than mine, then do it the way that satisfies you.

If you do not have perfect results the first time, just try again. It takes practice to obtain the desired results and to learn the tricks that make carving easier. I have thrown many pieces away, and still ruin one occasionally; don't be discouraged, therefore, if your first pieces aren't what you expect them to be.

Many carvers, especially beginners, find that they need ideas, patterns and instructions for carving and finishing. In the following pages, I will endeavor actually to show you how to carve and complete several figures. In doing them, don't forget to enjoy yourself.

Fig. 9. Project No. 1—Missouri mule pattern, using 1-inch squares.

Project No. 1 - Carving a Missouri Mule

TOOLS USED

KNIFE
SMALL V-TOOL
5-MILLIMETER GOUGE
6-MILLIMETER V-TOOL
6-MILLIMETER MEDIUM SWEEP GOUGE
1/2-INCH SHALLOW GOUGE

CARVING AN ANIMAL

An animal caricature is fairly simple, so we will start with a Missouri mule. He is looking straight ahead and has all four legs in a good firm standing position. For strength, and ease in carving, his ears are up. His tail is close to his body, actually touching full length. It is doubtful that any mule ever had a head as large as this one's, but an oversized head is part of his being a caricature and will make him more amusing.

Linden wood (or any other wood of your choice) may be used. The block I used was 6 inches wide, 6½ inches tall and 1½ inches thick, with the grain running the 6½-inch length, or with the legs. The use of the grain in this manner will make the legs stronger.

STEPS IN SAWING AND CARVING

First, trace the pattern (Fig. 9) on the block, then saw out as much as possible, using the band saw or jigsaw; if you do not have power tools, a coping saw will do just as well. A handsaw or a brace and bit could also be used to remove some of the excess chunks. Once this basic outlining is completed, turn the mule upside down and clamp him in the vise. With a coping saw or keyhole saw, make two cuts between each pair of legs about ¼ inch apart. On the back legs, saw only to the tip of the tail, or about halfway; on the front legs, saw to the beginning of the body.

Next, take the tip of your knife or a small gouge and cut these pieces loose. This will leave you room to work between the legs. Now the actual carving starts, and while you may begin anyplace you like, I will mention a few places where you will need to take the wood away. The head, when finished, will be about an inch thick, or a little less, so the wood on either side should be removed. The place where the neck enters the jaw and head will be about ¾ inch thick, and where the neck enters the body should be about ⅞ inch thick, so some wood should also be removed from these areas. The body will be the full 1½ inches thick at the rump and the lower part of the shoulders. The

shoulders will taper up to the withers (or the place where the mane begins) almost to a point. Round the rump and taper the shoulders, using your knife. As you progress, look at Figs. 10, 11 and 12 to see where to remove the wood. Many beginning carv-

Fig. 10. *Mule sawed to shape on the band saw.*

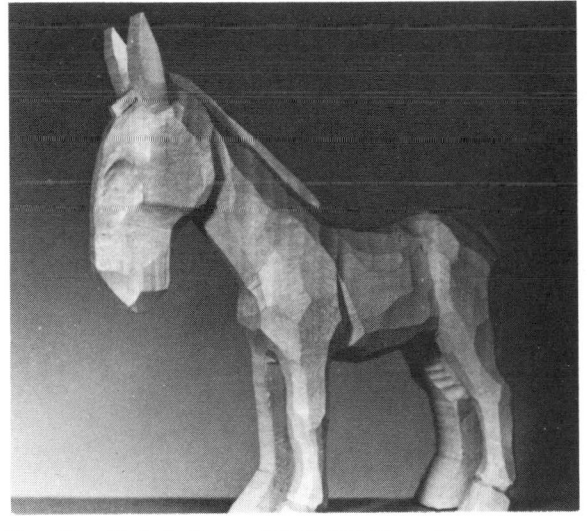

Fig. 11. *Mule half completed showing cuts.*

ers have a tendency to be afraid to take off wood, and their early works often have a square look. So don't be afraid of taking off wood, and be sure to get a nice rounded look to your carvings.

SMALLER POINTS

You must cut away on either side of the tail, leaving about ½ inch of wood. Now the legs can be carved and rounded (refer to Fig. 11). While the jaw

Fig. 12. Completed mule.

area is 1 inch thick, the muzzle is about ⅝ inch when the mule is seen straight on. The face is sunken from the eyebrows down to the nostrils. This may be done with a small gouge; I used a 6-millimeter medium sweep gouge. Finish the short mane and tail with a 2- or 3-millimeter v-tool.

Save carving the ears until last. They are the most delicate part, and may be easily broken if carved first. For the eyes I used a 5-millimeter flat gouge (about ³/₁₆ inch wide), making three cuts, to form a triangle, then cutting away the wood, leaving the eyeball between these. Lids may be added, and bags underneath, using a v-tool, your knife tip, or both. Nostrils were made with the point of my knife.

For the inside of the ears I used a 6-millimeter v-tool (a knife point may be substituted). Also, a 6-millimeter medium sweep gouge and a ½-inch shallow gouge were used to cut away the wood between the back legs near the belly. A smaller gouge and knife may be substituted for this ½-inch gouge.

VARIATIONS

The mule may be turned into a comical horse by shortening the ears and putting a horse's mane on it instead of the short, clipped mule's mane. You may even come up with something completely different. A friend, just beginning carving, started carving a horse, but ended up with an old hound dog; so don't despair if something like that happens.

After a little more practice, you may even vary the mule pattern. Try putting his ears back, make him braying, or perhaps kicking up his heels. You may make a stubborn mule out of him by putting him in a sitting position.

FINISHING THE MULE

Although you may use any of the finishes previously mentioned, I will show you how to paint your mule using the water-color method (see Fig. 12). It is a good idea to paint the mule at a time when you know you can finish the piece without having to stop. First, paint him almost entirely with raw umber, thinned with water to a medium brown shade, leaving out his eyes, muzzle and belly, which will be painted white. While the brown is still damp, start painting on the white, using white acrylic, also thinned. Work fast, so that you may blend the white and brown where they meet on the muzzle and belly and thus avoid the harsh line that would otherwise result.

You do not have to use a small brush when painting your carvings. I use a ½-inch flat show-card brush and a smaller pointed water-color brush. The ½-inch brush speeds up the painting, and after some practice with it, you will find you seldom need the smaller brush, except for very small places.

When painting large areas of a carving, your brush may be very wet. As you come near a place which will be a different color, use an almost completely dry brush, so your paint will not run into this area. When using a very wet brush, make certain you continue brushing while the paint soaks in to avoid streaking.

If you use the tube water colors, squeeze the amount you think you will need into a water-color pan or into a small jar lid. The paint you do not use will dry up, but you may still use it at a later date by adding more water. Once the acrylic is dry, you cannot use it again, so try to squeeze out only the amount you will need.

While using the white, go ahead and paint the eyeballs. Next, darken the mane, end of tail, hooves and the inside of the ears with black. With an almost dry brush (or better yet a toothpick) and a small amount of black, you may paint a pupil on each eye. Tint the lips and the inside of the nostrils with a small amount of red. Again, using the toothpick, paint a small red line on the bottom of each eyeball. Now the mule is ready to set up to dry.

When the mule is completely dry (after at least an hour, or being left overnight), you may cover him all over with umber antiquing. Wipe off excess with a clean, lint-free rag. You may think you have ruined your carving when you coat it with antiquing, but when the excess is wiped away, it will have the appearance of a very old wood carving, with colors toned down so they will not look too new or gaudy. If you use this method of finishing, your carving will still have the look of wood.

How to Carve a Head and Face

Faces are difficult for most beginning carvers, but they need not be; with a few basic cuts, a little practice, and extra-sharp tools, carving a face can be truly enjoyable. It is very satisfying to see a little square block turn into a face filled with much personality, under the deft strokes of your tools.

For practice, it is very helpful to take a piece of wood, 1¹/₂ × 1³/₄ × 12 inches, with the grain running the length, and try carving faces (Figs. 13 and 14). The 12-inch length will give you something to hold onto, and you may carve several heads before getting to the end.

To show the process of carving a head, two sequences of photographs are shown: Figs. 15-18 show the development of the head of a smiling fat man; Figs. 19-22 illustrate specific points in the process. The first step should be shaping the head (Fig. 15). Since the figure is to be smiling, we have left the piece a little wider than usual at the cheeks. When the head is shaped, you should start the carving by cutting ¹/₄ inch deep all the way across the face at the bridge of the nose (Fig. 19). A similar groove is cut all the way across at the bottom of the nose (Fig. 16). Now wood can be gouged out for the eye sockets and on either side of the nose, leaving the nose ¹/₄ inch higher than the surrounding areas (Fig. 20).

Cut some wood away from the eyebrows, so that they are arched upward. Remove wood from around the mouth area, so this remains raised. Since this face is to be happy, cut deep at the corners of the mouth area. Making sure your v-tool is very sharp, cut a crescent-shaped groove under the eye area and over each eye (Fig. 21); this will leave a little mound for each eye. Now cut some wood away between the mouth and the chin. A little wood may also be removed from either side of the chin. Take the v-tool and cut grooves for the hair line (Fig. 22). Next, cut wood away from the forehead to make the hairline slightly raised.

Carve the mouth (Figs. 17 and 18), then shape the nose and carve the nostrils. The eyes can now be carved; since the face is smiling, they will be squinting. If the eyes were to be carved open, they would give you an expression of delight. The eyes may be carved with a v-tool, then deepened with the point of the knife. Make some small grooves at the corners of the eyes (crow's feet), to help achieve the smiling effect.

Shape the ears and gouge a hole in each one. Carve the eyebrows, using a small v-tool. While you have the v-tool in your hand, you may also carve the hair. Since extra wood was left on the chin, you

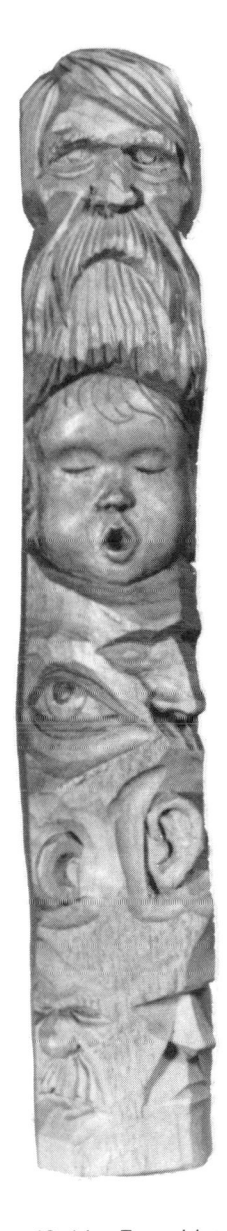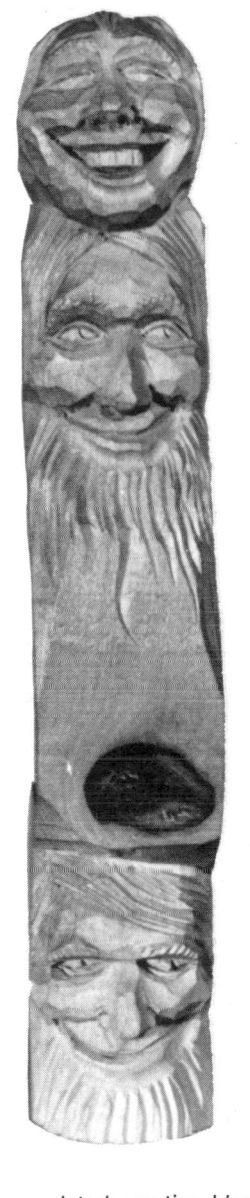

Figs. 13–14. Two sides of a completed practice block (front side, left; opposite side, right).

may now carve a double chin, by carving a groove with a gouge or knife under the regular chin, almost from ear to ear (adding a double-chin effect at the back of the neck too).

This will finish the head except for coloring or staining. Look closely at the photographs when trying this one. Faces take lots of practice, so don't give up easily. You may even practice just carving different shapes of noses, or eyes, or any feature which is giving you trouble.

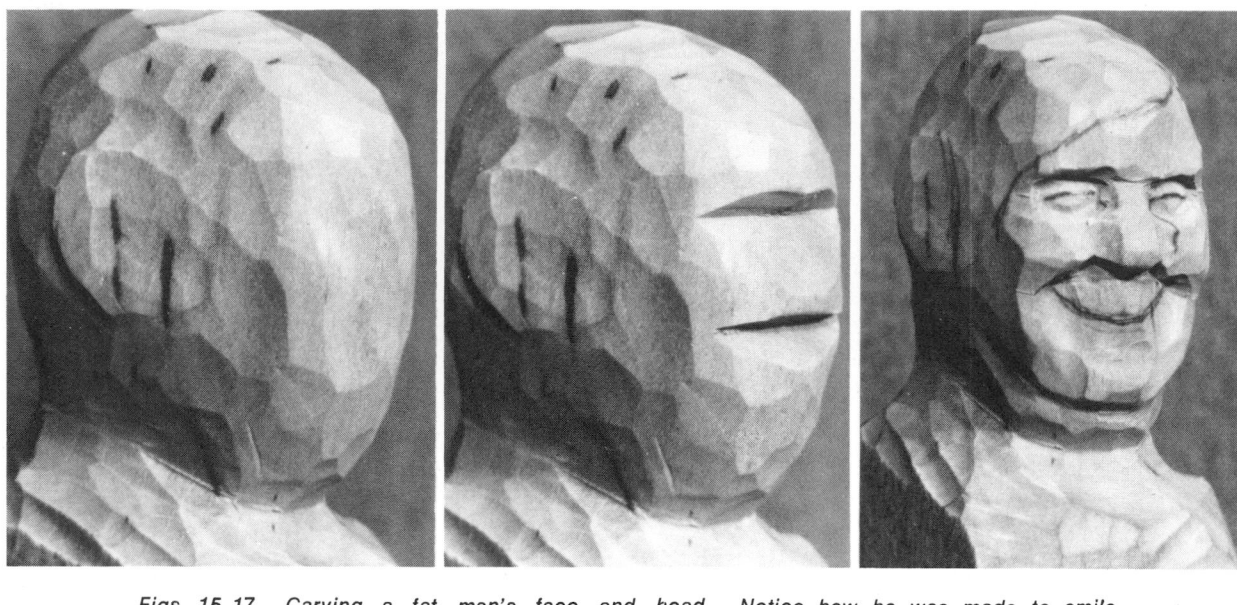

Figs. 15–17. Carving a fat man's face and head. Notice how he was made to smile.

Fig. 18. Completed face and head.

A CHECKLIST FOR FACIAL EXPRESSIONS

FOR A SMILING FACE: arched eyebrows (Fig. 23a), squinting eyes, mouth pulled up and back and the cheeks pulled up even with the bottom of the nose (which is greatly exaggerated on caricatures). Face and nose wider than usual.

FOR A SAD FACE: arch the eyebrows (Fig. 23b), carve heavy eyelids and make the mouth turned down and drooping.

FOR A CRYING FACE: squinted eyes (Fig. 23c), with crow's feet at the edges, brows furrowed and the mouth open and turned down.

FOR A LAUGHING FACE: cheeks high as in a smile (Fig. 23d), eyebrows high and arched, eyes squinting and mouth open, turned up and back.

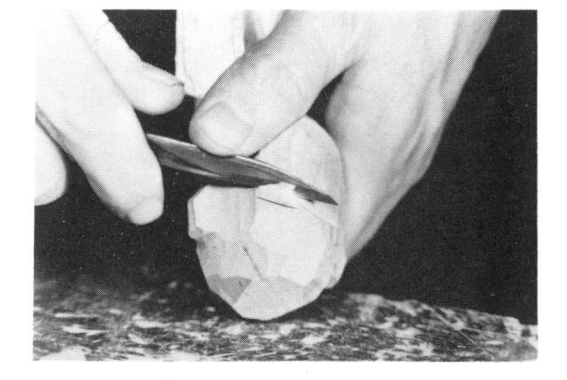

Fig. 19. The beginning of an eye.

Fig. 20. *Removing wood from the side of the nose.*

Fig. 21. *Making a small mound for an eye.*

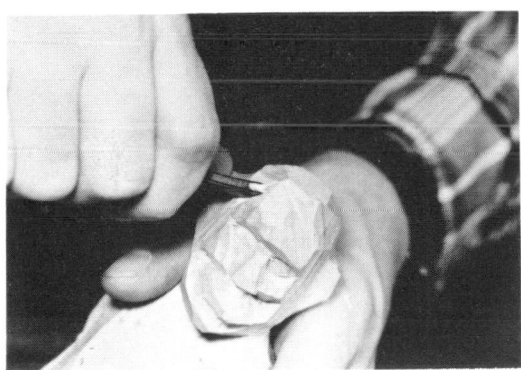

Fig. 22. *Cutting a groove for the hairline.*

VARIATIONS

There are many other expressions you may discover on your own, many being variations of the ones mentioned. An expression results from a combination of the features of the face. If you change one thing, such as the eyes, the mouth or whatever, you may get a completely different mood. If, for instance, you open the eyes on a crying face, you will achieve a look of anger. Being able to carve these various expressions and get the right one on a specific figure will come with practice.

I also find that by looking closely at other people, I learn much about facial characteristics. Keep a small mirror handy, and use yourself for a model to obtain specific expressions.

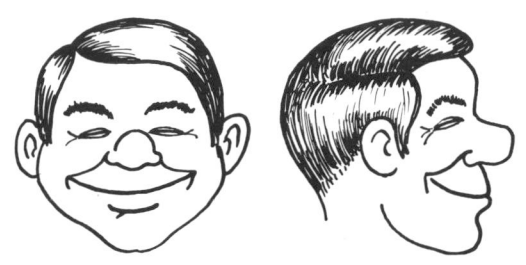

Fig. 23a. *A smiling face with arched eyebrows, squinting eyes, mouth pulled up and back, cheeks a little higher than usual and face a little wider than usual.*

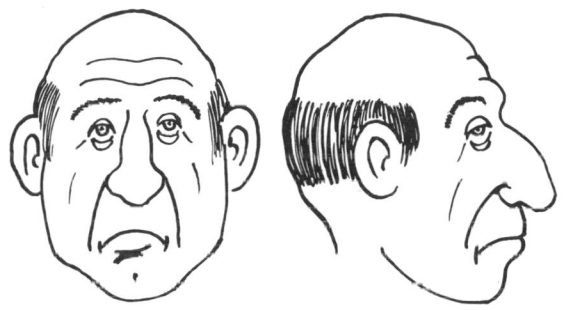

Fig. 23b. *A sad face with arched eyebrows, heavy eyelids and mouth turned down.*

Fig. 23c. *Crying face, eyes are squinted or tightly shut, brow furrowed, mouth open and turned down.*

Fig. 23d. *A laughing face, eyes squinted, mouth pulled up and back and open, with eyebrows arched. Tilting the head back a little will help with expression on this carving.*

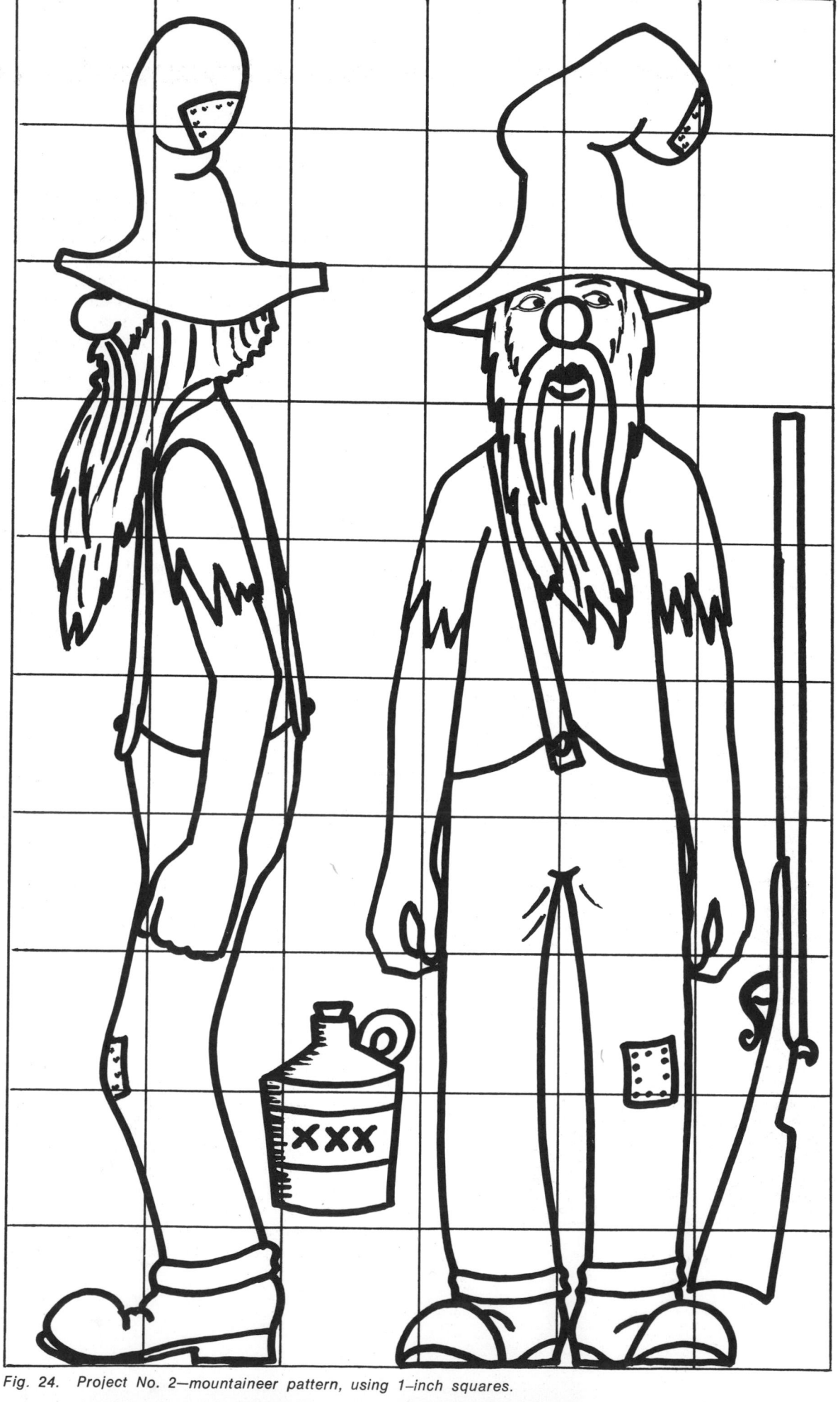

Fig. 24. Project No. 2—mountaineer pattern, using 1–inch squares.

Project No. 2 - Carving a Mountaineer

TOOLS USED

4- or 5-MILLIMETER MEDIUM OR DEEP GOUGE
6-MILLIMETER MEDIUM SWEEP GOUGE
SMALL V-TOOL
2-MILLIMETER FLUTER
1-INCH #3 GOUGE (for roughing out)
HANDSAW OR BANDSAW
COPING SAW
8-INCH C-CLAMP (or any size which will hold your work securely)

MOUNTAINEERS AS SUBJECT

Mountaineers are typical caricatures most often carved in the Ozarks region. While most Ozarkians don't look like this (Fig. 24), if you keep a sharp lookout while in the hills, you may think you see such figures.

For ease in carving, the mountaineer will be looking straight ahead and standing in a regular stance. His jug and rifle are generally carved from separate pieces, and added through holes carved in his hands. The hands themselves will be carved at his sides, in the position easiest for the beginner.

Fig. 25. Band-sawed mountaineer.

STEPS IN CARVING

We will start with a block 2 inches thick, $2^7/8$ inches wide and $9^3/4$ inches long, with the grain running the $9^3/4$-inch length. Since this carving will have no base, make certain your block will stand level before starting to carve. Trace or draw the side view on the block and bandsaw it, if possible, to the basic outline shape (if you do not have a band saw, refer to the chapter on "Roughing Out a Figure from a Block"). Now the front view is drawn on and the excess wood taken away from both sides. (While carving this project, refer to Figs. 25-27).

The next step is to take wood from the front of the arms. To help in this process, after the preliminary roughing out is completed, draw two lines on the front where the arms and body meet, from armpits to fingertips; this line will show you how deep to cut, using a 6-millimeter gouge or a large v-tool as in Fig. 7. Your roughing-out work is now finished, and you can see the figure starting to take shape.

Some carvers prefer to work all over a figure at once, skipping here and there. For convenience, however, it will be easier to list the next steps as if the work were being carved from the top (again, study the photographs for details, even if you make your carving different). Round the hat brim and make it floppy wherever you like. Also, work the top over, rounding it as well (always round each area before putting on the detail).

You can now start carving the head and face. Take special care here, and do your very best job. First, cut wood away from around the nose, letting this feature stand out. Next, round the face and back of the head. The neck, which shows at the sides and back, and runs underneath the beard in front, will be about $5/8$ inches wide. Leave small mounds for the mouth, mustache and the eyes.

DETAILS

Eyes are carved by first making a couple of small sockets with a knife or a 4- or 5-millimeter medium or deep gouge. The eyes themselves are now carved in these hollows, preferably on the small mound you have left in the center of each socket. Sometimes the knife tip works best on eye detail, sometimes the small v-tool, and often a combination of these two.

For the beard, taper it somewhat near the end, and carve slightly to one side near the tip, giving a pushed-over appearance. Beard, hair and mus-

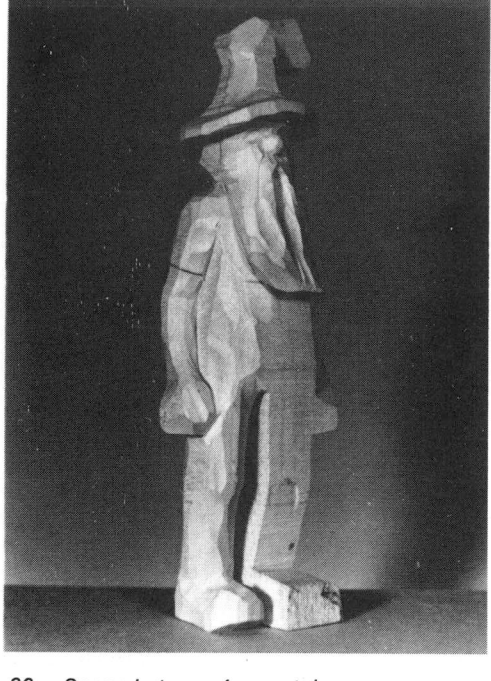

Fig. 26. *Second stage of mountaineer.*

Fig. 27. *Finished mountaineer.*

tache are made with a small v-tool, and can be straight or curved, depending upon your preference. My own preference is for gently flowing lines for hair and beard, and the v-tool, snaking its way along, is ideal for this. Remember, the v-tool must be properly sharpened for this, or one will have trouble. Occasionally, too, a piece of wood will be pithy or too soft.

Arms can be rounded, and a small groove cut where they meet the body to show that they are a separate part. Similarly, round the body and legs.

Hands are carved like mittens, complete with thumb, as a first step. After the hands are shaped, make three v-cuts and you will end up with four fingers. The first cut is made in the center of each hand, then one evenly spaced on either side of the first cut.

Next, the feet may be rounded and details added to them and other parts of your carving, such as cuffs, suspenders, ragged sleeves, patches, and buttons. For these small details I use the 2-millimeter fluter.

HOW TO CARVE THE JUG AND RIFLE

The mountaineer's jug and rifle aren't difficult to carve, but you should be careful as you will be working very close to your fingers on these pieces (see Figs. 24 and 27).

For the jug, use a small block of wood, approximately 1¼ × 1¼ × 1⅝ inches in size. First, carve it round like a dowel, tapering it slightly toward the bottom. Carve the neck to shape, leaving room for the handle. Carve the handle, and gouge or drill a small hole through it, so you can hang it from the mountaineer's hand with a piece of string or a thong. A couple of grooves around the middle, either with a v-tool or pocket knife, will make the jug look banded. On this band, carve some small XXX's to identify the moonshine inside.

For the rifle, you will need a piece of wood about ¼ inch thick by 6½ inches long. Draw on the side view, and cut to shape. Round the barrel and the stock. Now carve the trigger guard. Don't worry about carving the trigger on a rifle this small. Using a v-tool, cut a groove to distinguish the stock from the barrel. You may carve a hammer, if desired.

FINISHING THE MOUNTAINEER

Your mountaineer can be finished the same as the mule, if desired, using the coloring of your choice. My own carving is finished with stain and wax, in the manner outlined in the chapter on finishing.

I cleaned my carving by sanding it very lightly, and stained it with knotty pine, wiping off the excess stain. After it was thoroughly dry, a coat of paste floor wax was applied and buffed. One coat of wax will give a nice soft shine, but you may wax it as many times as you wish.

The rifle and jug can be finished in the same manner; then the rifle can be inserted into one hand and the jug tied into the other.

Your mountaineer is now complete and ready to put on a shelf or some highly visible place.

Project No. 3 - Carving a Hobo

TOOLS USED

6-MILLIMETER MEDIUM GOUGE
2-MILLIMETER MEDIUM GOUGE
3-MILLIMETER FLUTER OR MEDIUM GOUGE
3-MILLIMETER V-TOOL
AWL
HANDSAW
BRACE AND BIT
KNIFE (or other tools that may be substituted for any of these)

STEPS IN CARVING

To carve the hobo (Fig. 30), you will need a piece of wood 3 inches thick, 4 inches wide and 9¼ inches long, including the base; the grain should run the 9¼-inch length. Draw or trace the side view on the block, and band-saw it out, leaving a little extra wood around the head area, in case you wish to make a change (again, if you don't have a band saw, use your handsaw, as discussed in the chapter on roughing out).

A brace and bit will expedite removal of wood between the legs (Fig. 28); once the holes are

Fig. 29. Hobo partially completed.

drilled, a small gouge and mallet will take this wood out easily. With the piece clamped, gouge the wood from the sides of the legs, with one leg forward and one back. (Every project in this book will have different cuts to be made; some you will learn with experience, but the basics remain the same.)

After you have completed the roughing out, remove wood from the front and back of the arms. Then start at the top again, carving the head area (to the size of the hat brim), then carving the wood from under the brim, and rounding the face as you go. Make sure to leave a little wood for the ears as the head shapes up (refer to Fig. 29), and also mounds for the mouth and the eyes. When the head is carved to shape, the details may be added, as explained in the two previous chapters.

DETAILS

Carve the wood away from the nose, and gouge out sockets. Using the mounds you left, make the eyes squinting and the cheeks round; the mouth will be drawn up and back in a typical smile, cut quite deep at the corners. Ears can be formed with a small gouge by one or two pushes inward, and

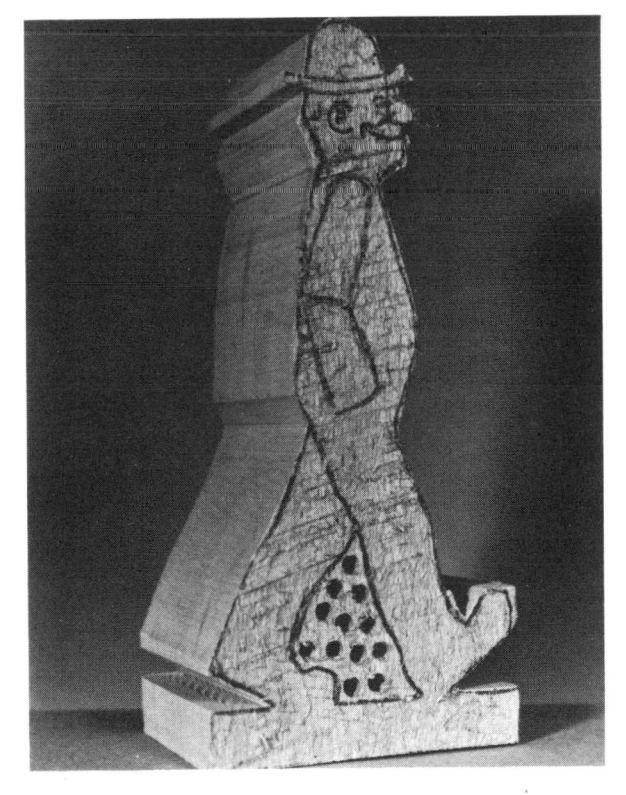

Fig. 28. Band-sawed hobo, with holes drilled between the legs to facilitate removal of wood.

Fig. 30. Project No. 3—pattern for hobo, using 1-inch squares.

Fig. 31. Completed hobo.

CARVING WRINKLES

Wrinkles are an important part of the detail on a carved figure. On small figures, these may be made with the knife blade, to give them an angular look; if a gouge or v-tool is used, the wrinkles may look like grooves in the wood instead. Save these tools for areas you cannot reach with your knife, or for wrinkles on larger figures.

On tight-fitting clothing, wrinkles will radiate from points of pressure, like elbows or knees. I generally carve a few radiating wrinkles at the crotch, both in front and back. There are always wrinkles where there are folds, such as the inside of the elbow. On baggy clothing, wrinkles and folds radiate from points where the garment is suspended, and there are also many folds where it is bunched up, such as baggy pants at the ankle. Generally, flat shallow wrinkles are best. Those carved too deep will again look like grooves rather than wrinkles. Observing folds and wrinkles on your own clothing will be a big help when carving.

FINISHING THE HOBO

We are going to finish the hobo as we did the Missouri mule, using water colors (or acrylics) and antiquing (see Fig. 31). Color will give your hobo a lot more character than using a stain. You may use colors of your preference, but these are the ones I used. The pants are brown, shoes and hat black, shirt and rope-belt yellow ochre, and patches vermilion. The hair and eyebrows are light black (use a very small amount of black, mixed with more water for a lighter shade), and the beard is a little lighter, so it looks like a three-day growth. For an older look, you may add tints of white to hair and beards occasionally. Blend small amounts of white in while the black is still wet.

Mix white and vermilion for the flesh, blending a little more vermilion on the cheeks, nose, tips of ears, and knuckles to give a rosy look. Blend well, so the vermilion will not look too harsh. Paint the base last as it will give you a good handhold while painting the rest of the figure. I painted the base green.

When thoroughly dry, apply umber antiquing and wipe immediately. Set up to dry, and watch this character closely, as he may head for the nearest railroad tracks.

you can pop out a piece of wood, thus forming a simple ear. Use the small v-tool to carve hair and to pop out little chunks to make whiskers. Do this rather haphazardly, so it will not look "worked-over."

Round the shoulders, and carve the arms to shape. The body may be rounded now. Outline the tie with a v-tool, and cut away the wood on either side, leaving it slightly higher than the shirt. The shirt collar can now be carved, with the tie going underneath. Next round the legs and shoes.

After you have everything rounded, you may put on the final details, such as patches, shoe soles, rope around the waist and toes sticking out of the forward shoe. It isn't necessary to carve the toes showing, but it does add a humorous touch.

Buttons are made with a 2- or 3-millimeter gouge. Patches are outlined with a v-tool and stitches added with an awl or an icepick.

Fig. 32. Project No. 4—cowboy pattern, using 1-inch squares.

Project No. 4 - Carving a Cowboy

TOOLS USED

6-MILLIMETER MEDIUM SWEEP GOUGE
2-MILLIMETER DEEP GOUGE (for buttons)
SMALL V-TOOL
LARGE 10-MILLIMETER V-TOOL
#11 10-MILLIMETER DEEP GOUGE
COPING SAW OR KEYHOLE SAW

STEPS IN CARVING

After band-sawing or cutting out the side view (see Figs. 32 and 33), clamp the cowboy to the work bench, backside down. In this position, cut the excess wood away from the front of the arms, referring to Fig. 7. I used a large wider-angle v-tool for this operation (mine forms an angle of 90 degrees when viewed from the end), but you may substitute a gouge or whatever you have. While the cowboy is clamped down, you may take the wood away from both sides of the head (Fig. 34).

Take a chisel or flat gouge and round the belly and chest, starting about where the fingertips will be, and going to the shoulder area. This will save you the trouble of rounding this area with your knife. At this early stage of the carving, use the largest tools that seem feasible; this will save you time and blisters.

Unclamp the piece, and looking from the top, draw the outline of the hat brim and whittle away the excess, leaving it oval-shaped. Looking from the front or back, draw the top part of the hat. With a small saw, you may saw this wood away, starting at the top and sawing down, then starting at the

side and sawing in, so that the pieces fall off, leaving the top part of the hat ready to be rounded.

Now either hold the piece in your lap and use a small gouge to take the wood away from the top of the brim of the hat, or else clamp the figure face down and take the wood out with a larger gouge. This leaves the brim curled up at the edges, authentic-looking for a cowboy hat. The hat can be rounded and finished to your own preference and the head rounded to shape. While shaping the head, cut up under the hat a little, to give more room to carve the face and ears.

Using a 6-millimeter medium-sweep gouge, cut the wood away from either side of the neck (consult the photographs, especially Fig. 35). After rounding the limbs and other parts, add the details. Again, refer to earlier chapters dealing with eyes, whiskers and the like, possibly changing expressions for this figure as explained in the chapter on "How to Carve a Head and Face."

FINISHING THE COWBOY

Although I used water colors on my cowboy, this time experiment with your own finish or colors. Since I have mentioned some of the basic ways to finish, you should have no trouble. If you use water colors, make up your own color scheme, or use any stain of your preference. By experimenting, and using your own imagination when carving and finishing, you will develop your own style. This is important, as you will not want your work to look exactly like someone else's.

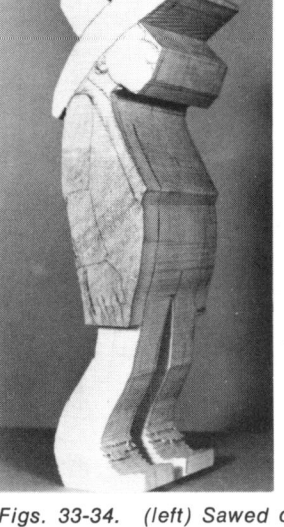

Figs. 33-34. (left) Sawed cowboy; (right) cowboy partially completed.

Fig. 35. Cowboy completed.

Fig. 36. Project No. 5—hill woman pattern, using 1–inch squares. Leave extra wood at the head when sawing out the blank, as the head is to be turned.

Project No. 5 - Carving a Hill Woman

TOOLS USED

6-MILLIMETER MEDIUM GOUGE
3-MILLIMETER MEDIUM GOUGE
1-MILLIMETER GROOVE
LARGE V-TOOL
HANDSAW
KNIFE

CARVING WOMEN FIGURES

Except for one detail, carving the hill woman is fairly simple (see Fig. 36). Her head, however, is turned to one side and that part of the carving will possibly be more difficult than heads of previous figures, who were looking straight ahead. Turning the head adds a lot to small figure carvings; otherwise, they often look as if they are standing at attention.

I chose a woman for this project showing the turned head, as she will have no beard or hat with which to contend. A profile of her face is shown in the pattern, in case you would rather have her looking straight ahead. You may want to try her looking straight ahead first, and attempt the turned head after a little more practice.

Choosing a feminine subject also gives you a chance to learn how to make pleats in skirts and carve women's hairdos.

STEPS IN CARVING

If you decide to turn the head of the hill woman, leave a block on top instead of sawing the profile. Before you start the hand work with your knife and small tools, clamp her to the bench on her back and carve the wood away from the front of the arms, using a gouge or a large v-tool (refer to Fig. 7).

To carve the head in its turned position, draw a top view on the block (roughly an oval) the way you want it turned (see Fig. 8). With the top view drawn, split the wood away from the sides of the head with a large chisel or flat gouge. To keep the shoulders from splitting along with the wood from the sides of the head, saw in at the shoulder line with your handsaw. When all the wood is taken away, you should have a block (turned to one side) sitting there on the sawed-out body (Fig. 37). Now round the head into the shape you want. Features may be carved on after the head is rounded. Usually the features turn out a little different from the original pattern: you may notice things you wish to leave out or change as you carve. It doesn't hurt to make

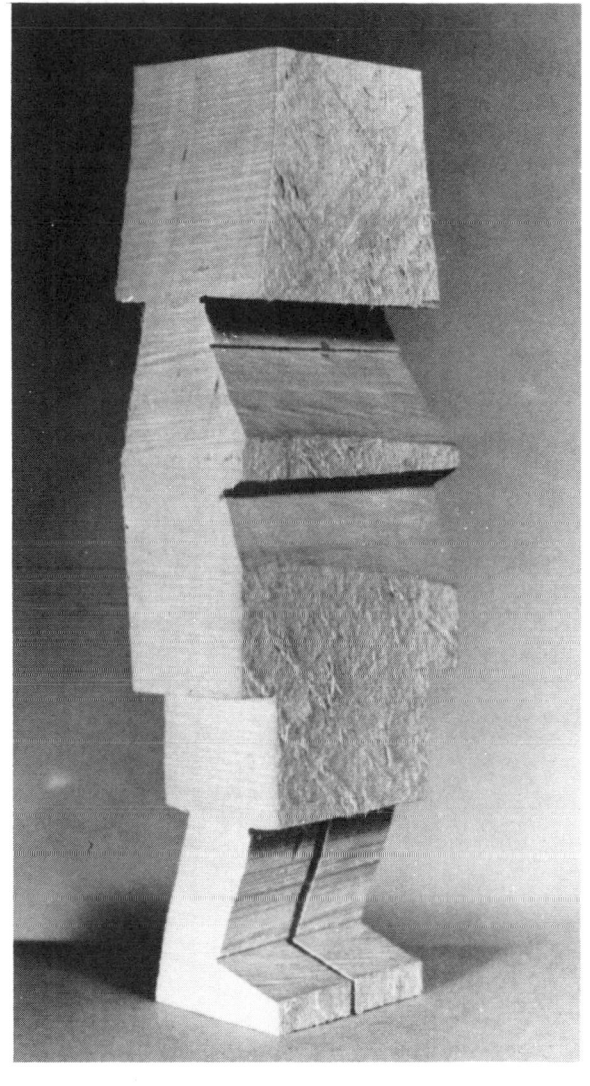

Fig. 37. Sawed hill woman.

the eyes a little larger on carvings of women or children.

DETAILS

After you carve the head, move on down and round the shoulders, arms and bosom. Carve the hands to shape, and add v-grooves for the fingers. If you bore through the hand with a 3-millimeter medium gouge, you may carve a flower, rolling pin, milk bucket or other appropriate items for your hill woman to hold.

Round the dress into shape, then carve in the pleats with a 6-millimeter medium gouge. The apron can be carved on now. Carve a bow where it ties in back at the waist line. You need not make a fancy bow, just two loops, and two loose ends hanging from a knot. Next, carve the legs to shape, referring to Figs. 38 and 39 for details. Carve the feet to shape before adding the toes with a v-tool. With a small 1-millimeter groove gouge, you may sign your piece by carving your name or initials on the bottom of one foot.

There are many types of hairdos you may want to try on your carvings of women. A lot can be done with hairdos and you will find this is a good area in which to experiment. Basically, the cuts for facial details will be those outlined in previous chapters.

FINISHING THE HILL WOMAN

Again, for my own carving I have used the water-color and antiquing method of finishing. I painted the dress vermilion and the apron white. Yellow-ochre makes the hair a dishwater blonde. Flesh is white mixed with vermilion, tinting the knuckles, cheeks and nose as before. The mouth on the hill woman should also be tinted a little more to give a rosiness. Eyeballs are white and pupils are brown.

Allow to dry thoroughly and antique.

Fig. 39. Completed hill woman.

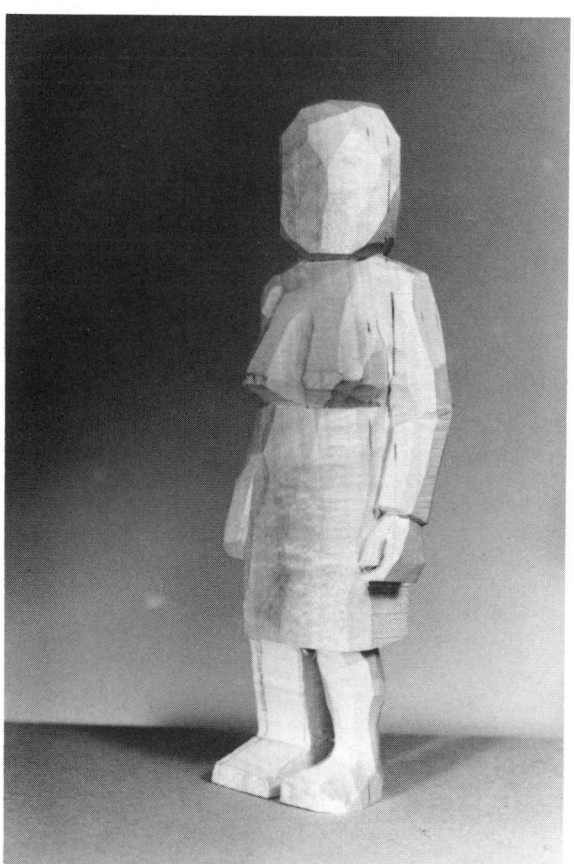

Fig. 38. Half–completed hill woman.

Project No. 6 - Carving Rufus and Sadie

TOOLS USED

    KNIFE
    6-MILLIMETER MEDIUM GOUGE
    V-TOOL
    2-MILLIMETER DEEP GOUGE
    AWL

CARVING THE SMALL FIGURE

Carving small folks is fairly easy, especially the way this couple is designed (see Fig. 43). You won't have to carve eyes and hands on Rufus, and Sadie's eyes are just dots or holes which can be punched in with an awl. There isn't a great deal of wood to be taken away, so most of the carving will be on the details. The band saw is always helpful, but on carvings this small, you can easily cut the profile with a knife.

CARVING SADIE

Sadie is made from a block of wood which is 1³/₈ inches × 1³/₈ inches × 3 inches, with the grain running the direction of the 3 inches. While carving her, refer to Figs. 40, 41, and 42. Draw or trace the side view on the wood and cut this profile with a band saw, jigsaw, coping saw or your knife.

After you have cut out this first view, take the wood away from the sides of the head, leaving a piece ⁷/₈ inches across when looking from the front. Now taper both sides of the figure, starting about where the elbows will be and going toward the shoulders. This will make the elbows the widest part, with the shoulders not quite so wide.

Draw the arms on the sides, and remove some wood from the front and back of the arms (refer to the photographs so that you take the wood away in the correct places). Take away some wood from

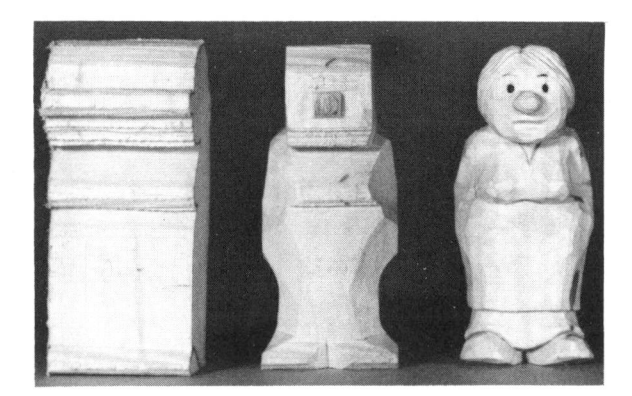

Fig. 40. Front view of Sadie in three stages.

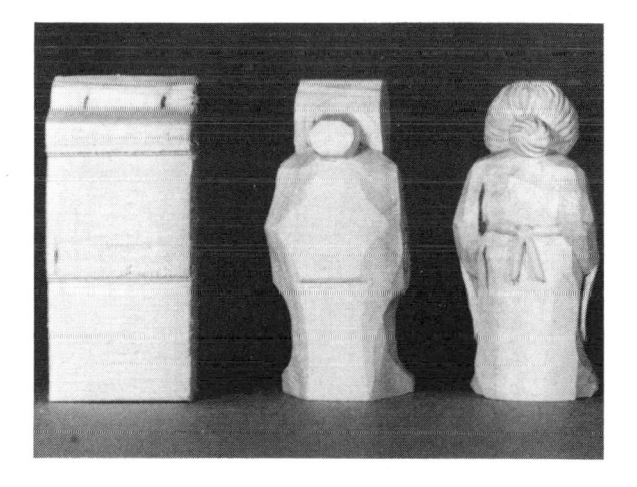

Fig. 41. Side view of Sadie in three stages.

Fig. 42. Back view of Sadie in three stages.

either side of the dress, below where the hands enter the apron. The dress may be rounded on all sides now.

Next, round the head, leaving the little piece for the nose. On the back of the head carve the wood away from either side of the bun and round it. In front, take a pencil and draw the hairline. After cutting a groove at the hairline, remove some wood from the face along this line, leaving the hair on a slightly higher plane than the face. A small groove on the top of the head will make a part in the hair. Use a small v-tool to make the lines in the hair.

Be certain to carve the face nice and round. Then add two dots for eyes. Take the awl and punch these two dots, then insert the point of a sharpened pencil and turn so it darkens the inside of the dots.

Fig. 43. Project No. 6—patterns for Rufus and Sadie, using ½-inch squares.

Fig. 44.   Front view of Rufus in three stages.

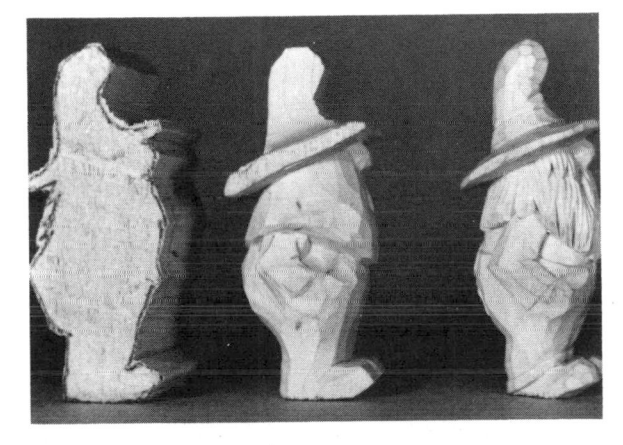

Fig. 45.   Side view of Rufus in three stages.

Fig. 46.   Back view of Rufus in three stages.

The mouth is just a small groove which may be carved with your knife or v-tool. You may add the eyebrows as you like, either drawing them on with a pencil or painting them on with a very fine line brush. Finish the arms to the proper depth, but don't go so deep that the body will be too thin. Finish rounding now wherever else it is needed. Cut a notch between the feet in front, and carve them, referring to the photographs. Add any other details needed, complete the knotted apron string in back, and the carving of Sadie should be complete.

CARVING RUFUS

Since Sadie was so easy, we should start on Rufus right away. He is from a block 1³/₈ inches × 1¹/₂ inches × 3¹/₄ inches, with the grain running the 3¹/₄-inch length. Rough out his profile in the same manner as Sadie, using either a saw or your knife blade. While carving Rufus, refer to Figs. 44, 45, and 46 frequently.

After the profile is roughed out, you may start carving on the front view. Start at the top with the hat, and cut the wood away from both sides of the top of the hat. Next, carve in underneath the brim of the hat, and round the whole head area, cutting up toward the brim. Go ahead and round the whole figure now. Cut a notch between the feet in front. Cut a groove where the bottom of the head and hair end, then cut some wood away from the body, leaving more wood where the beard will be. Cut away the wood from the sides of the nose, then round the brim of the hat. When you look from the top view, it should be nice and round.

Carve wood away from the arms, leaving them a little farther out than the rest of the body. After drawing the beard on with a pencil, use the point of your knife to cut away the bits of wood which are between the pointed tips of the beard. Do the same with the mustache and with the hair in the back. Round the top of the hat and add details, such as v-cuts for the whiskers and clothing.

FINISHING RUFUS AND SADIE

Rufus and Sadie have been left unfinished so that pictures could be taken in three stages. You may use any of the finishes described in this book, or you may use a finish of your own preference.

Fig. 47. Project No. 7—pattern for Bootsie the cow, using 1-inch squares.

Project No. 7 - Carving Bootsie the Cow

Carving Bootsie the Cow (Fig. 47) is a difficult and time-consuming project, but also one that is quite a bit of fun.

If you have completed all the projects thus far, you should be getting quite proficient with your carving tools and techniques. Therefore, I won't go into quite as much detail on Bootsie.

In the photograph I reproduce (Fig. 48), she was carved from basswood 2¼ inches thick by 5¼ inches high, and 7¾ inches long, with the grain running with the legs. The wood to be removed is much the same as the mule in Project No. 1. If you are still unsure of your cuts, refer to this project often. The neck is about the same thickness on the cow as the mule. The shoulders will taper up to almost a point. Save the horns until last as they may break easily. Since the hooves of a cow are cloven, you should run the v-tool right up the middle front of each hoof after it is shaped. Be sure to run the v-tool upward for these cuts. These grooves may be deepened by using the point of your knife. Bootsie's front feet are just a little pigeon-toed. This will add character to a caricature, so try yours this way if you like.

The place on the pattern which looks like a space between the tail and backs of the legs is in reality part of the udder, so don't cut through here. The tail touches the udder all the way down, except for about the last ¾ inch. Use a 6-millimeter gouge or similar tool to carve three grooves for ribs. The three lines on the pattern represent the center of each of these grooves.

Notice in the photograph (Fig. 48) that the teats on the front of the udder are angled outwards, while the two in back are straight down. Cows lay their ears back when bellowing and extend their head out and upward also. You may change the pattern so the nose is even higher if you like.

Her finish is in color: a reddish-brown body with white spots, pink nose and udder, and gray hooves and horns. After she is antiqued and well dried, paint her bell silver.

Tools used are the same as for the mule or those of your own choosing.

Fig. 48. Bootsie the cow completed.

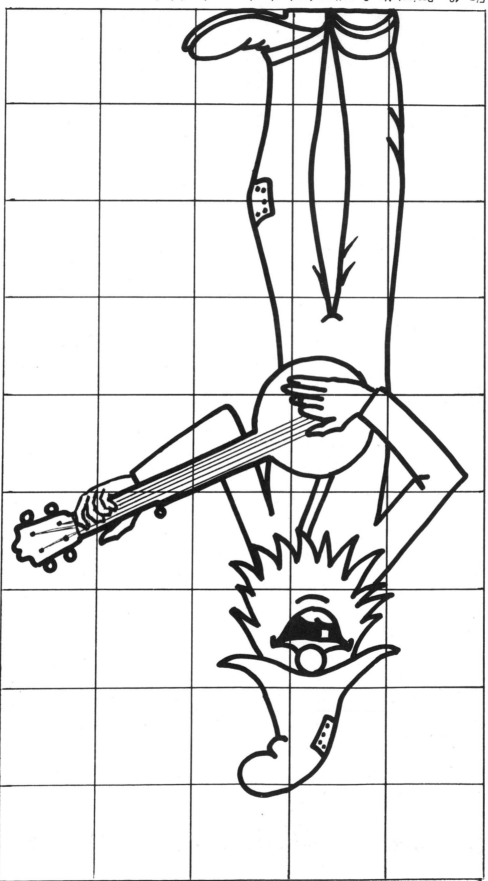

Project No. 8 - Carving a Banjo Player

After one has learned to carve a mountaineer, it seems but a brief step to showing one playing a banjo, that most American of all musical instruments.

The pattern shown here (Fig. 49) uses 1-inch squares. In the photograph showing my own carving (Fig. 50), 2-inch thick basswood was used. The figure stands 8½ inches tall and 4¾ inches at the widest part, which is from his elbow to the head of his instrument.

Carving procedure is much the same as for the Mountaineer in Project No. 2. The hands and angles of the arms are more difficult to carve on this figure. You must take off wood cautiously when carving the left hand on the neck of the instrument. This fellow is playing an old fretless folk banjo, so don't worry about carving cross grooves on the neck. The strings are represented by small v-grooves. Try to make them as straight as possible. I made four small holes with an awl to represent the studs where the strings attach for tuning. Tuning knobs are carved from the same piece of wood (Fig. 50), but you may carve and glue these in separately if desired.

Particular care must be given the enormously wide smile and glittering single tooth. The banjo player is glued onto the base. He was then stained, waxed, and polished.

Fig. 50. The banjo player completed.

Fig. 51. Project No. 9—pattern for "Ozark Trail's End," using 1-inch squares.

Project No. 9 - Carving "Ozark Trail's End"

This carving, called "Ozark Trail's End," is a take-off on a more famous work of art which you will probably recognize. One can only guess

Fig. 52. "Ozark Trail's End" completed.

whether the jug is full or not, but something has made the mountaineer (and his horse) doze off.

The pattern is supplied (Fig. 51) and uses 1-inch squares. The example I made (Fig. 52) from this pattern was carved from 2-inch thick basswood, is 8¼ inches high, and measures about 6½ inches from the horse's forelock to his tail. Since it's carved from a single piece of wood, it's a difficult piece to carve. The base could be higher if one used a larger piece of wood.

The procedure is basically the same for carving this figure as for the figures in the previous projects. First, you must cut out the profile, a task which can be very time-consuming if done completely by hand. Be sure to use your handsaw on the cross-grain cuts. A brace and bit or power drill is used to drill through the legs of the horse and in front and back of the man's arm. The trick of drilling to save time is fine, but be sure you drill straight through. If your drill leans to one side or the other, you may drill off part of an arm or leg on the other side.

Although the eyes are closed, you should still be sure and make a little mound on which to carve them. The horse's eyes are carved the same way: a little mound with sleeping eyes. Carving the man's suspender in front will be the most difficult part. It will also be difficult to carve the whiskers in back of the beard. This design could be changed so the man is leaning backwards with his beard lying on his chest. The carving would be less difficult in this position.

Note the exaggeration of the man's feet coming so far down. Normally they would only come to the horse's belly. His feet are bare, although you could carve work shoes or boots if desired. The man's right hand, which doesn't show, is hanging limp.

I used various small gouges for much of the carving on this piece; also, a knife and a 3-millimeter v-tool for the mane, whiskers, etc. Knotty pine stain was used for a finish, then one coat of paste floor wax which was buffed with a brush when dry.

Fig. 53. Project No. 10—pattern for "Revenooers," using 1-inch squares.

Project No. 10 - Carving "Revenooers"

The old fellow in this project is running away from the Revenue people, and the work is accordingly entitled "Revenooers." The pattern is shown (Fig. 53), using 1-inch squares; however, notice the difference in the beard in the pattern and that in the completed carving (Fig. 54)—this is an example of how the carver can change the design as the carving progresses.

Fig. 54. "Revenooers" completed.

He and his trusty mule are carved from a 3-inch thick piece of basswood, 7 inches high and 9¼ inches long. The base is carved from another piece of 3-inch thick wood, and the two are attached to each other by a piece of coat hanger. You will need to drill a small hole in the base and one in the mule's belly, each about an inch deep to insert the wire. This is done after all the carving and finishing is complete on both pieces.

First of all, trace the pattern onto the wood and begin removing the excess wood, either with a band saw or using the handsaw and gouge method described earlier in the book. Make the saw cuts across the grain and clamp the piece on its side onto the work bench to do your heavier gouge work.

With the profile cut to shape, you may continue with your knife and smaller carving tools. The tools you will need are the same as those used in earlier projects.

If you are going to design your own carvings, always take a little time to consider how easily certain areas may be broken. Breakage during carving can be practically eliminated by proper designing. Notice how the jug and tail help brace each other. This is an instance of planning ahead. In any area where something could be easily broken, it's a good idea to brace it with another object wherever possible.

"Revenooers" is a moderately difficult project, but very rewarding when completed. These little mounted figures are among my favorite subjects to carve. Also, as you progress as a carver, you will find it more satisfying to put a little action into your figures.

The eyes are important in this carving. Both man and mule should look frightened. Make the eyes wide open with the pupils small and centered. The white of the eyeball should be showing all around.

This old mountain man should have his feet toed in somewhat, and the mule's feet should also be turned in. The lower part of the reins and the tip of the tail may be saved until last as you will be cutting completely through the wood. They will be cross-grained in places and very easily broken.

Small gouges will prove useful on projects like "Revenooers" because of the many hard-to-get-at places where wood must be removed. A long, slender, well-pointed knife blade will be helpful in many areas on these finely detailed carvings.

This carving was stained with water colors and antiqued.

Fig. 55. This old cowpoke has a long mustache, but mainly I use this carving to show his furry chaps. Here you can make good use of a small v-tool.

Fig. 56. Standing hobo. Cigar and knapsack are carved separately. His eyes are open, while his mouth is smiling. His is a look of contentment, not at all out of place on a character as free as a hobo.

Fig. 57. This cowpoke is a tough one. Putting the thumb in his belt makes him a little different, along with the hair in his eye and his turned-up boots.

Fig. 58. This dragon, appropriately named "Snap," was designed from a picture in a newspaper. You can find ideas for many carvings in unusual places if you are on the lookout for them.

Fig. 59. Ordinary cowboy.

Fig. 60. A carving made several years ago for a gift. I used no pattern. Instead, the figure was just sketched onto the block, sawed, and carved. He is a good example of my earlier work, having legs which are too short, and arms which are too long. Of course, because he is a caricature, this does not matter too much.

Fig. 61. Two old mountaineers on their way home from the still.